PAPER ORPHANS

⚜ and Other Illegitimate Verse ⚜

James L. Thompson, Jr.

PublishAmerica
Baltimore

© 2007 by James L. Thompson, Jr.
All rights reserved. No part of this book may be reproduced, stored in a retrieval system or transmitted in any form or by any means without the prior written permission of the publishers, except by a reviewer who may quote brief passages in a review to be printed in a newspaper, magazine or journal.

First printing

PublishAmerica has allowed this work to remain exactly as the author intended, verbatim, without editorial input.

All characters in this book are fictitious, and any resemblance to real persons, living or dead, is coincidental.

ISBN: 1-60441-272-0
PUBLISHED BY PUBLISHAMERICA, LLLP
www.publishamerica.com
Baltimore

Printed in the United States of America

TABLE OF CONTENTS

"THE CREATIVE WRITER" 5
"LOVE LINES TO AN ICEBERG" 7
"PLEASE TUNE ME BACK IN" 8
"SCATTERED REFLECTIONS" 9
"RAINBOWS FOLLOW RAIN" 10
"SOLO" 11
"PREMEDITATED SEX" 12
"HEROES AND LOVERS" 13
"WALLS" 14
"FORBIDDEN FRUIT" 15
"PERCEPTION" 16
"A BLESSING OR A CURSE" 17
"TODAY I MET A GIRL" 18
"UMBILICAL CORD" 20
"THE GOLDEN WATCH" 21
"A PEACE OF TIME" 23
"STOP AND SMELL THE ROSES" 24
"THE WISDOM OF UNDERSTANDING" 25
"A BUTTERFLY'S WINGS" 26
"LOVE IS LIKE GLASS SLIPPERS" 27
"LIFE PARTNER" 28
"TODAY I SAW THE WIND" 29
"CAPTURING THE DAY" 30
"HEY MAN, I LOVE YOU" 31
"OLD FRIENDS" 32
"HOLIDAYS" 33
"CHILDREN AND FLOWERS" 34
"MY SIGNIFICANT OTHER" 35
"FREE SPIRITS: WHY DO BIRDS FLY AWAY?" 36
"MEN WHO CRY" 38
"WITH NEW EYES" 40

"DREAMS AND WISHES" 41
"WATERFALL" 42
"S P A C E" 43
"READING BETWEEN THE LINES OF LOVE" 44
"WHERE DO FIREFLIES GET THEIR LIGHT?" 45
"A SOMETHING-FOR-NOTHING WORLD" 46
"CONSEQUENCES" 47
"JUSTIFICATION" 48
"SHACK" 49
"HAIKU 4 YOU: SIGN OF THE TIMES" 51
"REINCARNATION OF A ROMANCE" 52
"BUFFALO SOLDIERS: FORGOTTEN HEROES
   REMEMBERED" 55
"WAY BACK WHEN" 58
"THE NEED FOR VALIDATION" 62

"THE CREATIVE WRITER"

I often write *creative* things to remind myself
that I am living, that I am here—now!
Because some days I am not sure,
not certain that this life isn't an emotional dream
gone wild after my *Creator created* me.
Yesterday I found a brand new penny faced down in a puddle of water.
I picked up the penny, made a wish, and kept if for good luck.
Why? I don't know why, I just did.
Not that I'm superstitious about this life or about living,
but that I wanted to see what would happen if my wish finally came true.
I wonder if it ever will. For I truly believe that:
The wings of a butterfly are merely the dreams come true of an optimistic caterpillar.
When I write, my hand births every word as if they will be my only descendants—
the sons and daughters miraculously consummated to remind others I once lived here.
They are the ones I've lovingly *procreated* with my own hands for posterity.

Yet I continue to write, feeling the need to *create* others to *validate* my existence.
And when I finish these living notes of life, I fold them into paper rocket ships and
carefully prepare them—my unique sons and daughters—for a short but fantastic ride
through a parental but lonely world made of paper clones.
I then sail them into the air, half-hoping that some day long after I'm gone,
someone will find the crumpled *paper orphans*, read them, and realize I once lived here.

Throughout all my years of living, learning, loving and listening, billions of words and thoughts have entered my mind and passed through my lips with different sensations and purposes. Some of these words made their way to pen and paper and *created* a life of their own. I don't know if these words were right, wrong, good or bad, but I do know they were true, real, honest and *creative*. Furthermore, they painted pictures that were quite introspective and reflected my innermost feelings exactly at the time they were *created*.
I am creative. I am a writer. I am a creative writer.

"LOVE LINES TO AN ICEBERG"

Trying to unthaw frozen affection
Is like licking a gigantic popsicle,
Confucius might say. What a protection!
Why must love be so cold? A mere obstacle
Blocking the way to a truthful heart
And causing one to feign what is felt.
A popsicle is still cold when torn apart
And sweet when it begins to melt.
But a person who is always cold
Will never melt anything but away
And probably alone; never to unfold
The mystery of those who stay
    In love rather than strive to be
    That part of the iceberg you can't see.

"PLEASE TUNE ME BACK IN"

Lately it seems we are on different wavelengths.
Our signals are strong but we are going in different directions.
Maybe it's me. Am I out of range?
If so, will you adjust my antenna,
Wiggle my dish, play with my remote
Or whatever?
Please tune me back in.

"SCATTERED REFLECTIONS"

Scattered reflections mean more than viewing
    thousands of pieces of broken glass;

Collectively, they mean having thrown about thoughts
    and fleeting images of past golden days.

A solid relationship can very well be
    shattered when troubles in paradise pass;

Trying to pick up the pieces after it's broken
    becomes a hard task to perform in many, many ways.

Tattered lives and battered emotions are often the result
    of fragile hearts made broken;

Even the love and memories of days gone by
    can not replace the hurt now felt.

Remembering that it was better to give than to receive,
    is only an adage that serves as a token;

For efforts in rekindling an unwilling candle are futile,
    if they, like wax, begin to melt.

Do scattered reflections ever reassemble themselves after being broken?

"RAINBOWS FOLLOW RAIN"

They say,
rainbows follow rain
but when someone special leaves,
nothing ever seems quite the same.

When someone special comes,
our heart opens up like a door
and pulls the welcome mat safely
on the inside.

But when someone special leaves,
that same heart shrinks
to the size of a pin
and sticks itself to bleed.

"SOLO"

At times we have to sing alone in order
to be heard above the others. But it's not
the song that we sing that will make us known,
but the way that we sing it. Not too soft and not too high.
Or not too low and not too loud.

Even though life may seem like a solo for some,
it is a song worth singing. For who can tell,
it may finally prove that you are in harmony while
everyone else is out of tune.

"PREMEDITATED SEX"

Murder and Love can both be
spontaneous, impulsive and premeditated.

Love can be murderous
and Murder can be lovely
if expertly done by professionals.

"HEROES AND LOVERS"

Heroes
are best remembered
by their incredible
feats;
Lovers
are best remembered
by their indelible
words.
Both are immortal!

"WALLS"

The treasure is now safe!
As far as the human eye can see,
An impenetrable wall encircles a well-guarded treasure.
Is it a Fort or a Fortress?
It makes no difference to the attackers.
This wall was built as a defense mechanism
Against those who trespass and plunder—
Against those who give pain instead of pleasure—
Against those who rob and leave the lights on—
Against those who…AGAINST EVERYONE!
Burning this wall with fiery old flames
Yields no instant admission.
Scaling this wall with intent to do malice
Provides only a rungless ladder to descend.
Smashing this wall with sticks and stones
Reflects no visible scars on its force field.
Robbed once before, this treasure will not be robbed again,
And this wall guarantees that it won't.
Built by a very shrewd but foolish architect,
This barrier not only keeps others out,
But it also keeps the treasurer hidden from other treasures.
Are they diamonds or fool's gold?
It makes no difference to the wall.

"FORBIDDEN FRUIT"

From afar I admired the beautiful tree
and I longed to get nearer for a better look.
From behind the fence I adored the luscious fruit
so I climbed the fence to get even closer.
The warning signs were all around
but I ignored them to get even nearer.
A piece of the forbidden fruit
broke loose by itself and rolled next to me.
I picked it up and held it
in my hands platonically.
With no intentions of eating it,
I began to crave a piece and then I took a small bite.
As I devoured the fruit, I became the fruit
and it became me — we were one.
From then on I was ripe with desire
and I longed to be with other forbidden fruit.
The only thing forbidden now is
my will to return to the innocence I once had.
I am the sinful, forbidden fruit
And I will be here forever.

"PERCEPTION"

Who would perceive life inside a peanut,
Or look to find freedom inside a shell?
Probably one who believes that honey is in a coconut,
Or the color of a rose does not determine its smell.
And what in him sparked HIS interest to make him see?
Possibly his belief and his humbleness,
Or maybe his sincerity,
Whatever HE had perceived, he went on to confess.
The life of the peanut was soon illuminated,
But freedom was still far behind,
Yet HIS spark of interest was communicated,
As it forever remained in his mind.
For just as the sheep of the shepherd are spread in herds,
He used the peanut (among other things) to spread HIS words.

(Written upon leaving the George Washington Carver Museum in Tuskegee, Alabama)

"A BLESSING OR A CURSE"

Why me? Why was I born to crucify
myself on paper for all the world to read?
Why must I shed my blood, sweat and fears
on paper for all the world to see?
I'm not sure if I were blessed or cursed when I was born—
born to be a writer.

"TODAY I MET A GIRL"

Today I saw a Girl —
young, pure and impressionable.
Warmly, her smile singed my soul
and her beauty made me reminisce
how it feels to be infatuated:
    It feels just like love…so right,
so genuine, so magical, yet the magic often
fades when the mysteries unfold.
    Flowers, candy, and kisses are initially
cherished above all, but even they yield when
true love does not exist.
    I suppose candid convictions are more
preferred than candied rhetoric, kindly coated
with sweet, illusive truths.

Today I met a Girl —
inexperienced, eager and optimistic.
Softly, she held my hand and her
touch made me wonder what makes life real,
what makes love real.
    If true infatuation is manufactured feelings manifested by

fickle emotions, then real love must be made of that which is
Divine: blind trust, faith and prayer.
　　An inexperienced love can rise to the top
when the teacher is the heart rather than the head.
　　I believe life seems more real, more worthwhile
when one heart is in tune with another.

Today I let a Girl—
loving, original and stable
enter my world through an invisible door.
Gracefully, she walked in and again
I placed the reins in my heart's hands.
　　Starting anew with a new love is never easy
when old hurt lingers freshly, but to start over is to
love again.
New faith gives way to new trust and old
　hurt becomes healed with forgiveness.
　　Although today I saw, met and let
a Girl singe, touch and enter my life, I
feel I have just discovered a new Lady.

"UMBILICAL CORD"

Matthew 19:6
speaks of a model marriage without divorce —
a modern day miracle to say the least.
Yesterday Adam's rib was enough to sustain Eve
after the serpent appeared in the garden
with the poison apple.
Today when the serpent appears,
all the ribs in the kitchen can't keep us from
cutting the umbilical cord — that vital lifeline which connects
Husband and Wife at the birth of a marriage.
Everyone knows a vowed marriage can only be severed by death,
but the serpent modernized and changed the shape of his
poison apples to the form of legal misnomers.
The red tasty ones are dubbed irreconcilable differences.
The delicious yellow ones are called incompatible lifestyles.
And the tart green ones are named non-commensurate
educations—
all equally poisonous but convenient alibis to legally sever
the cord when troubles appear.
Fortunately, Matthew 19:6
does not share the same legal opinion. It simply says,
"Wherefore they are no more twain, but one flesh. What
therefore God hath joined together, let no man put asunder."

"THE GOLDEN WATCH"

Time Watches Over Our Carefree Days of Infancy
    With Peace, Calm and Tranquility.

Our Invulnerable Adolescent Years are Lavishly Spent
    Without Stress or Worry and They Remain Forever Gold.

Yet the Precious, Quiet Moments of Maturity are Not
    Perpetual — They Only Last Until the Silence Breaks.

A Peace of Time That Eludes the Clock and Renews
    Our Youth is One That is Rare and Prime.

Like the Proverbial "Needle in a Haystack," It Seems
    Impossible to Find Until We Look Inside and Behold It.

This Inner Peace is Both Timely and Timeless —
    Its Silent Music Uplifts Our Spirit and Awakens Our Soul.

Nothing Escapes or Enters Our Mind When We're

Reflecting on a Piece of Time Suspended.

The Golden Watch Does Not Symbolize Retirement—
It Symbolizes the Full Circle of Our Youthful Life.

The Golden Watch Was Not Made to be Rewound or Reset—
Yet It Keeps Perfect Time by How Well We Live.

"A PEACE OF TIME"

The carefree days of newborn babies, so calm and tranquil,
    cleverly evade capture by staying suspended in time —

Thus a peace that eludes the clock and renews
    our youth becomes one that is rare and prime —

And, like the proverbial needle in a haystack, seems
    impossible until we look inside and behold —

This inner peace, both timely and timeless,
    gives us an uplifting and our spirit it awakes —

As we listen to the soothing music of every silent thought,
    it harmonizes our soul and makes us feel sublime —

With our eyes closed and our mind open,
    nothing escapes or enters during this period when dreams unfold —

Quiet times cannot be bridled or broken into pieces,
    but to know oneself inside is all that it takes —

"STOP AND SMELL THE ROSES"

Roses sometimes take on different names
    in certain stages of their development,

But a native rose by any other title
    is still a native rose, regardless

Of the changes in climate, location or
    other conditions foreign to its environment.

And although thorns may line their flowery path,
    carefully bloomed roses are still very special nevertheless.

Some say a flower in its ripest hour
    is too late for us to fully appreciate.

Too many rose gardens lie barren in the sun,
    for too soon we forget and put away our hoses;

Furthermore, roses will inevitably die and wither,
    but not before they beautifully communicate

Their delicate meaning in our lives. When they're in season,
    we should always stop and smell the roses.

"THE WISDOM OF UNDERSTANDING"

Sometimes…
Unspoken words say more than realized
And spoken words say less than actually meant.
But when the wisdom of Silence and Understanding touches lips,
Words disintegrate and matter very little.

"A BUTTERFLY'S WINGS"

Butterflies don't start out with wings —
    they tend to acquire them through a metamorphosis

As caterpillars, they tread and toil the earth
    in an humble fashion until they earn such things —

Although every butterfly was once a caterpillar,
    not all caterpillars become butterflies —

If a caterpillar is not steadfast and sturdy,
    somewhere along the transformation his dream dies —

The wings of butterflies are merely
    the dreams come true of optimistic worms —

Like getting a second chance in a new life,
    the caterpillars are reincarnated but on new terms —

They now must use their wings to symbolize
    the rewards that hard work and faith bring —

And how the Spirit replenishes the humble
    and teaches the butterfly to sing —

No better creature is there
    than the blessed butterfly —

To teach us about life on earth
    and life beyond the sky —

"LOVE IS LIKE GLASS SLIPPERS"

When Prince Charming presented Cinderella with the glass slippers,
he symbolically placed his heart in her hands.
Fragile, rare and crystal clear,
the glass slippers perfectly reflected his love.
The light that sparkled so brightly through the slippers
was only matched by the light that sparkled in her eyes
when she first saw them.
For in that moment, Cinderella knew the value
of what the prince had given her.
When she eagerly slid her feet inside the slippers
and found a perfect fit, it felt like magic.
And so is it with love and friendship.
It is equally rare to find someone with whom we click.
But when we do click with someone, we find that the
friendship is both delicate and crystal clear.
And as magical as it may seem, we'll
never be the same again.
In love and in life,
when you find a shoe that fits,
simply wear it.

"LIFE PARTNER"

In Life
Everyone needs a partner—
Someone to talk to
Confide in
Walk with
Believe in
Hold onto
Someone to—
LOVE.
In this life
You are my
Life Partner

"TODAY I SAW THE WIND"

Not far from where I was sitting in the sun,
I saw a miracle happen right before my very eyes.
The wind seemed to be playing merry-go-round in a sand pile
and a bee was darting and gliding overhead like a small plane.
As the bee dove toward the grassy ground,
a boyish image faintly came into view;
it's hand fanned the bee back up toward the sun.
Breezing off after it, the childish wind raced and
escorted the bee over the tops of the trees.
And they disappeared beyond the sky.
What a miracle! Who would believe me?
Today I saw the wind take time out to play with a bee,
and I wondered if again I would ever see anything
else so breathtaking.

"CAPTURING THE DAY"

Oh! If only I could make this day last forever
And take it out when I need it again...
The wind is blowing freely through to my soul—
The sun is shining brightly through to my soul—
The rain is showering lightly through to my soul—
    I feel so very good, so alive, so blessed!
And I'm cherishing every second of this day's rare gifts.
If every day was like this one, we wouldn't have to worry
About trying to capture the days and keep them forever.
But every day already is special and rare;
why don't we feel good all the time?
Today I feel very good.
    What day is this?

"HEY MAN, I LOVE YOU"

Yesterday I wrote my Best Friend a letter
and signed it, Yours truly.
After I mailed it, I wondered why I didn't sign the letter,
With Love.
After all he is my Best Friend and I do love him.
Then I wondered if my stubborn male pride had gotten in the way
and made me too ashamed to tell another male I love him.
But he's not just another male, he's my Best Friend.
I suppose I was trying to find another way to tell him I love him
without actually saying I love him so that my meaning would not
be misconstrued. But how can love be misconstrued?
Why didn't I just say what I mean?
We've been friends for over twenty years. When we were younger,
it was easier, but I never told him then either. I may never get another
chance or a better chance to tell him than now.
After all he is my Best Friend and I do love him.
Today I'll write another letter and this time I'll say,
Hey man, I love you.

"OLD FRIENDS"

Things of old
are very rare
to those who care
to collect them.

Friends of old
are very rare
to those who dare
not forget them.

"HOLIDAYS"

The older we get, the less holidays like Easter and Christmas seem.
The farther we get away from home, the more we reminisce
about Easter egg hunts and Christmas tree lights.
But these special days mean much more than eggs and gifts.
With Christmas we celebrate the birth of Christ.
With Easter we celebrate the resurrection of the
Holy Spirit and the reclamation of our faith.
Through self-denial, Lent and Palm Sunday, we
relinquish those things that we can do without and
we surround ourselves with lillies, palms and other
symbols of reverence, peace and love.
But the true spirit of these holidays lies in the way they affect
our personal lives by fixing our hearts and by preparing our souls
for the next day.
In truth, the older we get, the more holidays like Christmas and
Easter should seem.
The farther we get away from home, the less we should reminisce
about yesterday's holidays, for we should always possess the spirit
of the holidays in our hearts today.

"CHILDREN AND FLOWERS"

Children
are like flowers;
they grow best
when watered with
Love.

"MY SIGNIFICANT OTHER"

What's significant about us
Is that you belong to me and
I belong to you, forever.
No matter what society says,
We were meant to be.
I am yours and you are mine,
S I G N I F I C A N T L Y.

"FREE SPIRITS: WHY DO BIRDS FLY AWAY?"

Broken perches, changing climates, and hungry minds
are general reasons why birds take flight.

    Seeking strands of straw to build their nest or
food to feed their minds, they sometimes land near us.

    Possibly birds are like us. And if they are, I'm
sure there are other things that make them soar to higher heights.

    Although they don't stay long and they're not ours to keep,
it's nice to see one land in our backyard; thus,

    Birds connote freedom, just like children, heaven
and flags on poles.

    Birds are meant to wander, to fly solo, and to
frequently change their homes.

    Like them, we are often compelled by an inner
drive to reach our goals.

And when we do, yesterday becomes a pathway to much greater domes.

No one can surely know if the birds' flights are ever in vain,

Or if their searching will lead them back this way to our door.

But for our sake, let's pray that the birds will come back to us again,

And that they will take us with them, wherever, on their next soar.

"MEN WHO CRY"

Men who cry
must have hearts made of sponges;
men who don't
must have hearts made of stone.

Men who cry
display an uninhibited courage
to feel compassion and empathy
for human frailties.

Men who don't shed tears
were cast in that prehistoric mold
set eons ago by those who lie
and by those who are near-extinct.

Men who cry
reveal a God-given emotion
which separates them from inhuman creatures
who lack the ability to show sorrow.

Men who cry
can hear the cries of other men
and make them know that it's
natural to taste the tears of heaven.

Men who cry
are men like me.
I am a man who cries
and feels for love and friendship.

Men who cry
are men of a chosen lot.
As we cry, we will inherit the wind
to gently blow away our tears.

"WITH NEW EYES"

When I first saw you, I didn't notice YOU;
    I saw only a familiar face attached to a fatigued body
Like mine: worn, weary, and withdrawn.
    In you, I saw a mirror image of myself more than I saw
What represented you. But now, after knowing you better,
    My vision has been enhanced.
With new eyes, I see you as an humble friend who
    Unselfishly puts others before your own special needs.
I see you as a soft candlelight that touches others
    With your care and causes a chain reaction similar to
A Domino Effect.
    I can see through you, to your soul, and know that
Your heart is pure; I can actually feel your aura as it
    Encircles your face and permeates your body.
And I see you tomorrow as you change only to remain
    The same, realizing that love is a renewed faith in life.
With new eyes, I see you, I see me,
    Walking together, hand-in-hand, heart-to-heart,
Looking forward to the day that we become ONE.

"DREAMS AND WISHES"

Dreams and Wishes
most often come true
when the Mind and the Heart
are joined with Faith.

"WATERFALL"

With every single drop
I stop
to reflect on what you
meant to me and how I
wish you would've stayed.

Your calls turned into
letters and your letters
turned into notes—
reminding me not to forget you
"with love."

Is there any way at all
to cushion the water's fall?

"S P A C E"

Sometimes
I need mine
and you need yours,
I understand.

Occasional breathers
are good for any
relationship
so that neither one
ever feels crowded.

However, I hope the
breathers are brief,
for I wouldn't want
anyone else to crowd my
S P A C E.

"READING BETWEEN THE LINES OF LOVE"

GIRL, I'VE HEARD THAT A
   (I'm only saying
PICTURE PAINTS A THOUSAND WORDS.
   or painting this letter
WELL, THAT MAY BE TRUE IN
   in a realistic form of words
SOME CASES, BUT THIS PICTURE
   to simply tell you that
PAINTS ONLY THREE WORDS.
   I Love You.

IT'S KIND OF HARD FOR ME
   It's not too difficult
TO SAY WHAT'S REALLY ON
   to tell you this
MY MIND, SO I'M HOPING THAT
   because I'm hiding my feelings
YOU CAN READ BETWEEN THE LINES.
   between the lines of love.

THIS MAY BE A SILLY WAY TO
   Now that you've heard me once
TELL YOU THAT I CARE ABOUT YOU
   I'm going to tell you again—
BUT YOU'VE GOT TO ADMIT—IT'S A SMART WAY.
   I Love You.)

"WHERE DO FIREFLIES GET THEIR LIGHT?"

On almost quiet
crickety summer nights
of dimly-lit skies
that resemble both solitude and despair,
tiny bursts of light "flicker" about like
"flashes" of new inspiration or like
ideas of hope conveniently appearing
so we can SEE that all is never lost.
Where do fireflies come from?
Where do they get their light?
I wonder if fireflies ever experience burn-out?

"A SOMETHING-FOR-NOTHING WORLD"

The Human quest for an endless favor
Without offering a hand to repay the deed done,
Makes this world four-seasoned without savor.
That selfish myth deceives almost everyone,
But there are some who are still chivalrous,
Untainted by the thought of money and material things
Being obtained through means that are often hideous
And with the desire to truly earn their wings.
Still there are those who seek the light load and
Low risk street, never to give, only to receive;
But soon Judgment will come and we all must stand
On our own two feet and begin to heave
    Our way into the Coalyards or the Vineyards as payment,
    For something for nothing is only a figment.

"CONSEQUENCES"

I once watched an eager little boy
launch a little paper boat in a beautiful lake.
The little boat peacefully waded along
until it came upon an unexpected waterfall.
When it reached the waterfall,
the little boat fell out of view
and the little boy cried.
That whole scene made me think of the word, "Consequence" —
that which naturally flows from a preceding action
or condition; result; a logical conclusion.
You see, the boy, the boat, the lake and the waterfall
were each operating as created to be.
The boy's natural wonder made the boat
sail on the waters with an un-chartered course
until it reached its logical conclusion — the waterfall.
If the boy or the boat had control over the lake
or the waterfall, things may have been different.
I don't know what happened to the little boat,
but I like to think that it landed safely upright
and continues its sail to this day
until it reaches another logical conclusion.
Life is full of consequences
but all of them don't have to be
painful or fatal.

"JUSTIFICATION"

Just-i-fi-ca-tion.
A very strange word with an even stranger definition:
The act of justifying
or the state of being justified;
that which justifies.
Four different variations of the same word
to say what?
Some feel that they need it.
Others ask for it just because.
The rest don't give a damn or
they don't feel they need it.
Justification is like a condom —
a thin layer of perceived protection used
before engaging in activities that may
effect or correct
the level of sensitivity received when
being seduced by your own fears or
when flirting with the Mother
or Father of insanity.
After all, crazy people don't need any justification.
I'm with them.

"SHACK"

Your life has plenty of shattered panes and
    cracked walls, but you still remain;
Your body is not as strong but you
    still stand;
Sometimes you feel empty and unwanted but
    you still love;
And although things get cloudy and rain may
    appear, the sun still comes out.
For through all the shattered pains in your heart
    and water in your eyes, you still SEE.
Through all the loss of strength in your body
    and weariness in your feet, you still WALK.
And through all the holes in your life and cracks
    in your soul, you still PRAY.

Remember: "He forgives all my sins. He heals me. He ransoms me from hell. He surrounds me with lovingkindness and tender mercies. He fills my life with good things! My youth is renewed like the eagle's! He gives justice to all who are treated unfairly.

He is merciful and tender toward those who don't deserve it; he is slow to get angry and full of kindness and love. He never bears a grudge, nor remains angry forever.

He has not punished us as we deserve for all our sins, for his mercy toward those who fear and honor him is as great as the height of the heavens above the earth." (From Psalms 103)

"HAIKU 4 YOU: SIGN OF THE TIMES"

Ice caps melt,
a global warning.
Penquins swim.

Bottles of water
look like WMDs.
Airport security.

The Big Easy.
Family reclines on top
of sinking home.

Bombs attack Iraq.
Stock market crashes
with same sound.

"REINCARNATION OF A ROMANCE"

I really didn't want to go to the party I had been invited to attend. "C'mon, you'll have fun. Plenty of food and girls," they all promised, but I just wasn't ready to be around a lot of people again. I wasn't in the mood for fun or food and I didn't want to meet another girl. All I wanted was Kathy back, but I knew that was impossible. Every time I'd mention her name, my friends would all remind me that it had been a year since she'd left and it was time for me to move ahead.

"She didn't just leave," I said. "She's dead and she's not coming back, ever."

"Okay, but there's nothing you could have done. She had an accident and you can't go on feeling sorry for yourself forever. Let it go man. Let it go. There's no reason to live the rest of your life dying," they said.

Deep inside I knew they were right. Maybe that's why I decided to go to the stupid party anyway. But a moment after I arrived I wish I hadn't come. All get-togethers are alike to me. Same ol' stuff. The house was jam-packed with guests I didn't know and the speakers were vibrating off the wall with dance music. The guys huddled along the walls rehearsing the lines they planned to use on the girls, and the girls were running in and out of the ladies room, giggling and rehearsing their responses to the anticipated lines they hoped to hear. It seemed everybody came to party except me.

Pushing my way through the crowd, I made it to the refreshment counter. I chomped on a few chips and gulped down a glass of punch just to be sociable. Looking at my wristwatch, I decided to give it five more minutes. Then I got the strangest sensation I was being watched but I didn't know by whom. My eyes scanned the room to see if I could spot anybody looking at me. From across the room I saw a cute girl quickly look away when she thought I was looking at her. I waited until she looked back in my direction and I watched her eyes dance away to avoid my stare. She was beautiful. When she looked again our eyes seemed to be in sync. My eyes penetrated her skin to look at her shy, illusive soul. It was so weird and uncanny. My heart felt funny and it started to develop a crush. She made me wonder if I'd gotten mixed up in another world somewhere with people I've known from a different life. That was my first time seeing her but I could have sworn I'd been in love with her before.

Trying to get closer to her without being too obvious, I casually made my way in her direction through the crowd. Although the house was full, no one else saw our private stares or distant touches. In a surprise moment we were actually meeting at a very common place. A place no architect could design with wood or stone, but a very special place somewhere deep inside our hearts. When we finally got close enough to touch, we quietly stood and squeezed hands, not wanting to let each other go. Holding her generated so much warmth and electricity inside me. Everyone else seemed to disappear and nothing else mattered.

Never uttering a word to each other, we danced to a slow song and our feet were already familiar with the steps. Our bodies moved like magic and our hearts kept perfect time like a two-faced clock. With fingers that moved like they belonged to a concert pianist, she touched my face and caused my heart to play. I smelled her perfume and recognized the fragrance; the way she smiled let me know I was right. She then rested her head on my shoulder and I secured my arms around her waist. I had never felt so strange in all my life. It was both eerie and wonderful to feel like I was falling in love all over again with someone I'd just met. She knew me and I knew her and it was anything but platonic. We were far too familiar with each other for this to have been a coincidence. When the music stopped playing we kept dancing, swaying only to the melody inside our hearts. No one else seemed to care that we continued; now they all knew we were in love.

I wasn't sure if it was proper to kiss her on the first date, but I knew I'd kissed her before. The way she looked at me let me know it was alright. When we kissed our lips parted as if to allow our spirits to rise and reunite within each other. We became a part of each other, yet separate. At first the kisses were soft and wet and then they became slow and long. When my lips finally left her mouth, I kept my eyes closed. I was imagining an instant replay, trying to make this moment last forever. When I opened my eyes, she had the same look of confidence in hers. We both knew.

What a great party! After it began to break up, I sensed it was time for her to go, but no way was I going to lose her again. I touched her face to assure her I would never leave her, and she smiled to let me know she knew. We stood and stared in each other's eyes. It was so strange. It seemed we only needed a few hours to renew a lifetime of loving each other. I turned and waved at my friends, thanking them for inviting us and then we clasped hands and walked outside. I unlocked the door to my car and held the door for her to get in. She got in and we cruised off into the moonlight, sitting extremely close to each other and feeling very good. Driving over the hill in my orange-colored VW Beetle, we must have looked like two lovers leaving an enchanted ball in a huge, magic pumpkin. Then I knew we had been given a second chance and our love was reincarnated.

"BUFFALO SOLDIERS: FORGOTTEN HEROES REMEMBERED"

April 22, 1994 will always be a day to remember in Dallas, Texas and around the world. On this day, some "forgotten heroes" were proudly remembered 128 years after an 1866 Act of Congress (July 28, 1866) authorized the formation of six African-American regiments in the peacetime army prior to the Civil War. These six all black military units encompassed two calvary (9th and 10th) regiments and four infantry (38th, 39th, 40th and 41st) regiments. The black infantrymen were subsequently merged, renumbered and renamed as the 24th and 25th Infantries. These soldiers were respectfully nicknamed "Buffalo Soldiers" by the Native Americans probably because the black soldier's "wooly" hair reminded them of the sacred buffalo known for its raw strength and fierce courage.

The U.S. Postal Service enshrined the Buffalo Soldiers in memory with the issuance of a 29-cent commemorative stamp. But the Buffalo Soldiers commemorative stamp is not just another stamp with a black face. The stamp, designed by Mort Kuntsler of Oyster Bay, New York, was officially dedicated in Dallas by Marvin Runyon, the Postmaster General and CEO of the U.S. Postal Service. Paying his respects by wearing a western hat and a bolo tie,

Runyon unveiled a 12-foot high replica of the stamp commemorating the black calvary units that helped settle the West. The stamp colorfully depicts a lesson in history that is virtually invisible in history books.

The honored guests of the ceremony held at the Hyatt Regency Dallas at Reunion were keynote speaker U.S. Navy Commander Carlton Philpot, who is also Chairman of the Buffalo Soldiers Committee, and former Buffalo Soldier, SGT Mark Matthews, Sr., U.S. Army Retired, 10th Calvary, 1917-1947. They both paid tribute by wearing the hats and scarves of their early counterparts. SGT Matthews was visibly moved when the stamp was unveiled and when Philpot vowed to continue the efforts to have the Buffalo Soldiers commemorated at the Smithsonian Institute and in history books by the year 2000. After being presented with a special Buffalo Soldiers plaque by Runyon, SGT Matthews gave his stamp of approval by striking a pose in a soldier's "salute" to the audience.

Over several decades, Buffalo Soldiers served in forts throughout the U.S., including Texas, Arizona, New York, California, Louisiana, Oklahoma, Montana, Utah, Nebraska, Virginia, Vermont, and Kansas. Fort Scott, Fort Larned and Fort Leavenworth in Kansas were a few of the strategically-important posts protected by Buffalo Soldier regiments. In fact, Fort Larned was the key to protection of the Sante Fe Trail.

The attitude of the U.S. Army toward the black soldiers during the Civil War and the Spanish-American War may account for the reason why the Buffalo Soldiers story is considered a "missing page" in American history. It is said that the Buffalo Soldiers endured cruel hardships and routinely received inferior food, equipment and horses. However, the Buffalo Soldiers received the highest number (18) of Congressional Medals of Honor and had the lowest desertion rate of any Army regiment from 1867 to 1898. In addition to engaging in fights with Native Americans, they confronted outlaws, desperados, protected stage and railway lines, strung telegraph wires, guarded frontiersmen against bandits and cattle rustlers and "rescued" Teddy Roosevelt and his Rough Riders during the Spanish-American War.

In his book, The Negro's Civil War, James M. McPherson documented that, "Although over 178,985 black men enlisted in the Union Army during the Civil War and fought in 449 engagements, of which 39 were major battles, and in spite of the fact that approximately 37,300 black soldiers died wearing Union uniforms, their military accomplishments were never fully appreciated, especially by the military leaders." And William H. Leckie wrote in his book, The Buffalo Soldiers, that "There were many white officers who looked upon an assignment with black soldiers as undesirable. So strong was the prejudice against black soldiers that some white officers preferred to take a lower rank in a white regiment as an alternative to duty with a black regiment. George Armstrong Custer, when offered the rank of lieutenant, turned it down, hoping to get an appointment in a white regiment."

Although history has not been mindful of the accomplishments and contributions of many unsung African-American heroes like the famous Tuskegee Airmen, the Negro Baseball League, or the Buffalo Soldiers, at least now the U.S. Postal Service is trying to right some of the wrongs. Ironically, the Buffalo Soldiers, who were expected to lick the boots of other regiments, are now being licked by Americans everywhere, every time they mail a letter.

"WAY BACK WHEN"

Ever wonder what happened to the black power fist and the peace sign? Were they just fads that faded along with afro puffs, platform shoes and popcorn shirts? I shall never forget the stir caused by Afro American Olympic runners Tommie Smith and John Carlos when they raised their black-gloved clenched fists over their heads during the playing of the U.S. national anthem at the 1968 Summer Olympic Games in Mexico City. The gesture later got them banned for life by the International Olympic Committee (IOC) and expelled from the Games. The IOC obviously viewed the gesture as rebellious and militant. However that gesture was a very proud and historic moment for a lot of blacks. Why? Because we viewed the extended fist as an extension of the Civil Rights Movement that was well under way by then. And it gave birth to words like "Afrocentricity." Later boxing heavyweight Joe Frazier began his two year reign as champ by using his powerful black fist to knock out Jimmy Ellis. I imagine at that time his victory song was James Brown's "Super Bad."

In the 70's, I remember feeling especially soulful and proud as I strutted down the street like a peacock. After I'd spend all day picking out my afro to perfection, I'd put on my big apple hat, my red, black and green polyester jumpsuit and my platform shoes. I felt both clean and funky at the same time. And when I met another Brother or a Sister, I'd raise my arm, clench my fist and say, "Right On!" And I'd always get a mirrored response from the Brother or the Sister acknowledging my presence. Those were the days when being-black-was-being-black and we were not afraid to greet each other in public.

During that time James Brown's pulsating black national anthem, "Soul Power" electrified the record players at all the house parties and gave us a surge of ethnic pride. And all over the streets, people in my neighborhood were echoing the words to Marvin Gaye's "What's Going On?" and "What's Happening Brother?" Some of us were even "digging the scene with a gangster lean" as we cruised in our cars with "sunroof tops and diamonds in the back" while we jammed to William Devaughn's "Be Thankful for What You've Got." Of course, we didn't have much but we were very thankful for what we had.

In those days blacks were not the only ones "rebelling" against the conservative norm with long hair, wild clothes and loud music. Young liberal whites created the "flower power generation" and made freedom and fashion statements with beads, bell bottoms and bushels of flowers. Flashing the two finger peace sign all over the place, some whites even sported their "permed" version of the afro. If there were indeed a racial awareness or an awakening taking place, both blacks and whites were experiencing it together. In 1970 four students were fatally shot by National Guardsmen during an antiwar demonstration in Ohio at Kent State University. The first Earth Day debuted and suggested that "Environmental Protection" would become a global issue. All the music from the now legendary Woodstock concert along with Tommy James and the Shondells' "Crystal Blue Persuasion" and Don McLean's "American Pie" will always be associated with the time when all of us were discovering our American heritage and learning about each other in the process. The common denominator then was the confusing Vietnam Conflict that we all tried to make sense out of to no avail.

And when the peace sign looked like it was on its way out, it resurged in another form during the Nixon administration. Nixon grew famous for raising both hands and displaying two peace signs to create his victory symbol; he was being "hip" in order to win the election. By the time Jimmy Carter took office, the country seemed to be striving toward change with an assorted racial make-up. The bicentennial year (1976) brought experimental "biracial study groups" that re-examined the race situation and tried to find solutions to the age-old problems. Still a distant galaxy away from racial harmony, the racial make-up of the country was beginning to look different, and it was a lot different than it had been just ten years earlier. The American Dream was no longer seen as a "Once Upon A Time" fairy tale; some believed the long struggle was beginning to pay off for whites and for minorities. Of course, history did not record the next twenty-five years as anything to brag about regarding the end of racism. There were still struggles and there were still "pay-offs" but that was then, this is now...

Last week at work I was in a crowded "Corporate America" elevator with some other prominent brothers and sisters. To my surprise everyone remained tight-lipped and no one spoke to each other or even acknowledged the presence of each other. When I did manage to catch the eye of a young Brother standing next to me, I smiled and said "Hi!" He only looked away and pretended he didn't hear me. Later that day I was walking downtown and I ran into a former classmate I hadn't seen in years. I recognized her before she saw me. When we approached each other I said, "Hello Sherry!" She looked away and kept walking as if she didn't hear me. I said, "Wait, Sherry. It's me, James." Then she stopped, turned around and said, "Oh, James I didn't recognize you. I thought you were just some Brother trying to hit on me."

How did we get to this point? Whatever happened to blacks greeting each other in public with the Black Power fist? The Black Power fist was a part of our cultural legacy that is slowly disappearing if not dying along with other vestiges of black history. Luckily, some of the importance of the teachings of historic leaders like Malcolm X briefly resurfaced during the release of Spike Lee's movie about our slain hero. During this time blacks (and some whites) everywhere could be seen wearing the "X" logo on caps, shirts, jackets, shoes, eye wear, etc. Unfortunately, the "X" fad has now faded too; we'd be hard-pressed to still find the "X" logo on anything anymore. Marvin Gaye's "Inner City Blues" (1971) and Prince's "Sign of the Times" (1986) provide musical similarities and food for thought to the notion that history repeats itself; they were both "right on" when they sang about the degradation of our society and ourselves as we fight a losing war against drugs, black-on-black crime, and the re-establishment of the black family.

I recently heard that the afro hairstyle is making a comeback. At first I asked "Why?" And then I realized it's just a fad, a phase of life that will come and go as rapidly as "Superfly" and "Shaft." And it's alright for the afro to make a comeback as long as we remember that the old saying, "Afros don't make Negroes" is probably true and always will be.

"THE NEED FOR VALIDATION"

Miracles happen daily. I once read about a New York City beggar who won over 50 million dollars in the lottery. When asked how she was going to handle her new found wealth, she smartly replied, "First, I'm going to get a job and become a respectable citizen."

"A job?" asked the dumbfounded reporter. "But why? You're rich now. You don't need a job."

"But being rich is not like having a trade," she said. "I want to have a real job so I can feel like I belong to something. I can't write homeless person or millionaire in the box reserved for occupation on my tax form."

Preposterous, you say? Well, not really. The need for human *validation* is a real thing. Although somewhat unexplainable, humans do possess an irrepressible need to belong to someone or something. It is a nondescript feeling but one so strong and important that a streetwise beggar-turned-millionaire felt that she needed an occupational title in order to be valid. In spite of her wealth, she still has the common need to belong.

"Will you please *validate* my parking ticket?" said the middle-aged man to the hotel clerk. "Of course, Mr. Smith," said the clerk as she stamped his ticket. Mr. Smith tipped his hat, said "Thank you" to the clerk, and ran off with a modest smile. Perhaps Mr. Smith or the desk clerk hadn't realized it, but more than the parking ticket had been *validated* during that short exchange. Each received a generous acknowledgement of their existence pertaining to their respective positions. The attention and respect that we receive from others help to give our lives meaning.

From an infant holding tightly to his daddy's thumb to a suckling calf clinging to her mother's breast, all creatures seem to have the need for *validation*. The infant is an infant and the calf is a calf, both separately and logically identifiable by their differences and their likenesses. In a ferocious world of identity crises and distorted values, there is no substitution for the feeling of self worth. To have *validity* in our lives is to have truth and to feel successfully alive. No matter if you're a bartender, a professor, a plumber or a beggar, you should feel secure enough to be true to your station until change effects it.

None of us were created to be beggars or millionaires, but we were all cut out to be workers in the melody of life who should be able to pursue every endeavor without fear of failing and becoming losers. After all, success and failure depend on the perception we have of ourselves at the time. If you feel you're a success, you are; if you feel you're a failure, you may fail unless you change your perception.

From preschoolers to college grads to grandparents, we are constantly tasked to decide what we are to become to help give our lives more meaning. Being compatible with and accepted by our peers is an important incentive behind the exhaustive search for *validity*, yet even before we've been accepted by our peers, we still need to be accepted by those three little inner peers—the *Me, Myself and I* of the soul.

Years ago my 89 year old grandmother had the urge to go back to school to get her high school diploma or GED. Amused by the idea, my father discouraged her from pursuing that goal by pointing out she was too old to go back to school. My sisters and I thought it was pretty funny too; we all giggled when we imagined

Granny sitting in a classroom wearing an apron. Granny smiled and never brought up the subject again. A year later Granny died without obtaining her diploma. I had forgotten about that until I was recently watching a Senior Citizens Tournament on the TV show, "Jeopardy." The "old" people featured on that episode were in their eighties and nineties but were incredibly smart. Uncontrollably, a tear fell from my eyes for Granny. I knew then that she had felt unfilled and *invalid* at not getting her diploma. And to think, we made fun of her when she attempted to pursue it. Since then I swore never to make fun of anyone's pursuit of happiness again, no matter how odd it seems to me. Live and let live so we all can feel *valid* is my new philosophy of life.

By trade I am a law enforcement officer now, but I've been a teacher, a salesman, a youth counselor, a construction worker, a dish washer, etc. In each job I felt a strong sense of self worth, although my true longing is to some day be a writer. I don't exactly know why other than it's what I feel I need in order to be *valid*. Money does not seem to play a major role in this urge I have. Throughout the years I've written many papers, poems, articles, essays, short stories, etc., but I still wonder if I have what it takes to become a successful writer. "Success"…there's that word again. Like the beggar, Mr. Smith and Granny, I long to have *validation*.

"Thanks for *validating* my ticket," said the young man as he handed his ticket to the parking attendant and sped out of the garage into the roaring traffic of the city where miracles happen daily.